# DK eyewonder
# Oceans

LONDON, NEW YORK,
MELBOURNE, MUNICH, and DELHI

**Written and edited by** Samantha Gray
**Designed by** Mary Sandberg,
Janet Allis, and Cheryl Telfer
**Publishing manager** Mary Ling
**Managing art editor** Rachael Foster
**Jacket design** Chris Drew
**Picture researcher** Nicole Kaczynski
**Production** Kate Oliver
**DTP designer** Almudena Díaz
**Consultant** Sue Thornton
Thanks to Sarah Walker for editorial assistance

### REVISED EDITION
#### DK UK
**Senior editor** Caroline Stamps
**Senior art editor** Rachael Grady
**US editor** Margaret Parrish
**Jacket editor** Manisha Majithia
**Jacket design development manager**
Sophia M. Tampakopoulos Turner
**Producer (print production)** Mary Slater
**Producer (pre-production)** Rachel Ng
**Publisher** Andrew Macintyre

#### DK INDIA
**Senior editor** Shatarupa Chaudhuri
**Senior art editor** Rajnish Kashyap
**Editor** Surbhi Nayyar Kapoor
**Art editor** Isha Nagar
**Managing editor** Alka Thakur Hazarika
**Managing art editor** Romi Chakraborty
**DTP designer** Dheeraj Singh
**Picture researcher** Sumedha Chopra

First American Edition, 2001
This American Edition, 2015
Published in the United States by DK Publishing
4th floor, 345 Hudson Street
New York, New York 10014
13 14 15 16 17  10 9 8 7 6 5 4 3 2 1
001—196636—02/2015

A catalog record for this book is available
from the Library of Congress.
ISBN 978-1-4654-1852-4

DK books are available at special discounts when purchased in bulk for
sales promotions, premiums, fund-raising, or educational use. For
details, contact: DK Publishing Special Markets, 4th floor, 345 Hudson
Street, New York, New York 10014 or SpecialSales@dk.com.

Color reproduction by Scanhouse, Malaysia
Printed and bound in China by Hung Hing

Discover more at
**www.dk.com**

# Contents

# Ocean zones

Oceans are divided into three zones, according to how far down sunlight reaches. To see in which zones creatures live, look for the red arrow in the picture below.

*Schools of fish, such as these silver snappers, swim in the sunlit zone.*

*Octopuses and squid live in all the ocean zones, including the twilight zone.*

### Sunlit zone

A red arrow pointing to the top area of this picture indicates sea creatures living in the sunlit zone. Sunlight reaches down to about 650 ft (200 m) deep. Most sea creatures live in sunlit water. Sunlight reaches through shallow seas and the upper waters of the open ocean.

### Twilight zone

A red arrow pointing to the middle area of this picture indicates sea creatures living in the twilight zone. Light becomes dim below 650 ft (200 m). The twilight zone reaches from here down to about 3,300 ft (1,000 m) deep.

## Fishy facts

● The deepest ocean is the Pacific, followed by the Atlantic, then the Indian. The Arctic is the shallowest of all the oceans.

● Many sea creatures depend on ocean plant life for their food supply. Plants need sunlight to grow.

● Coral and kelp only grow in sunlit seas.

*Deep-sea hatchet fish have lights along their bellies and tails that glow in the dark.*

*There is little food in the midnight zone, but the fangtooth's huge mouth allows it to vacuum up anything that comes its way.*

## Midnight zone

A red arrow pointing to the lowest area of this picture indicates sea creatures living in the midnight zone. No sunlight reaches below 3,300 ft (1,000 m), so the midnight zone is pitch black and freezing cold. The deepest parts of the ocean may be more than 13,000 ft (4,000 m) deep. This far down is known as the abyss. There are also trenches where the ocean is deeper than 20,000 ft (6,000 m).

# The blue planet

Oceans cover more than two-thirds of the Earth's surface. In this vast underwater world, many sea creatures live together, often hidden beneath the waves.

The Pacific Ocean covers more than one-third of the Earth's surface.

Gulls swoop down from the sky to scoop up a fishy snack.

### Fishing for food
Oceans are a source of food for seabirds, who fly or swim in search of fish.

### Sea turtles
There are many types of sea creature, including reptiles such as turtles. These have to rise to the surface to breathe. They breathe air through their nostrils.

Green turtles live in the warm waters of the Atlantic, Indian, and Pacific oceans.

## One big ocean

If you traveled in a boat, you could sail to every ocean and sea because they all join up. It could be said that there is really only one vast ocean.

## Plankton

The sunlit ocean teems with tiny life-forms called plankton. These are a vital food source for many sea creatures.

From space, the Earth looks blue because water covers so much of its surface.

## Breathing through blowholes

Whales are mammals. Unlike fish, they cannot breathe under water. They surface to breathe air through their blowholes. Blue whales are the largest mammals of all.

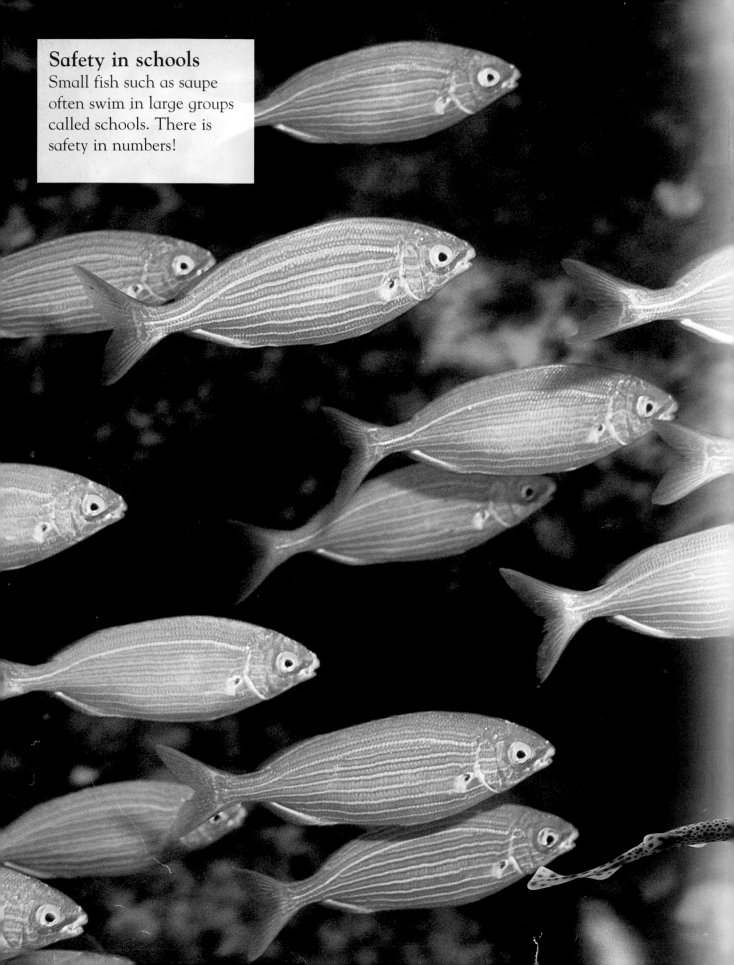

**Safety in schools**
Small fish such as saupe often swim in large groups called schools. There is safety in numbers!

# What is a fish?

All fish have gills for breathing under water and fins for swimming. Fish also have their own suits of armor! Most are covered in overlapping scales like tiles on a roof. Some just have extra-tough skin. They are slimy so that they can glide swiftly through water.

## How fish breathe

On land, oxygen is in the air. Water also contains oxygen. Fish gulp water and run it over their gills. Oxygen passes through the gills into the fish's blood.

## Super senses

Fish can hear, smell, and taste. They have taste buds in their mouths, fins, and skin. This polka-dot grouper swims head down while prowling for food.

*Muted color camouflages fish in the open ocean.*

*Fish often have excellent eyesight.*

*Opening to gills*

*Shapes and sizes of scales vary in different fish.*

## Swim like a fish!

Fish swim like snakes wriggle. Their bodies form S-shaped curves. Most fish use their tails for the main push forward. A few row themselves along with their fins.

*Lesser spotted dogfish*

*Dogfish wiggle from side to side.*

# Fantastic fish

Fish can be weird and wonderful! They vary in size from tiny sea horses to giant manta rays. Some have unusual shapes that help them to hide or scare off predators.

### Prickly beauty
Lionfish have striped bodies to warn away other fish. Any predator that bites a lionfish will be pierced by poisonous spines.

*Manta rays flap with wide, winglike fins and glide through the water.*

### Gentle giants
The vast, flat bodies of manta rays blend in with the mud and sand of the seabed. Despite their size, manta rays are gentle creatures. They eat mainly plankton.

### Hidden on the seabed
Stonefish change color to blend in with the seabed. They have spines on their backs for protection. Each spine injects a deadly poison if touched.

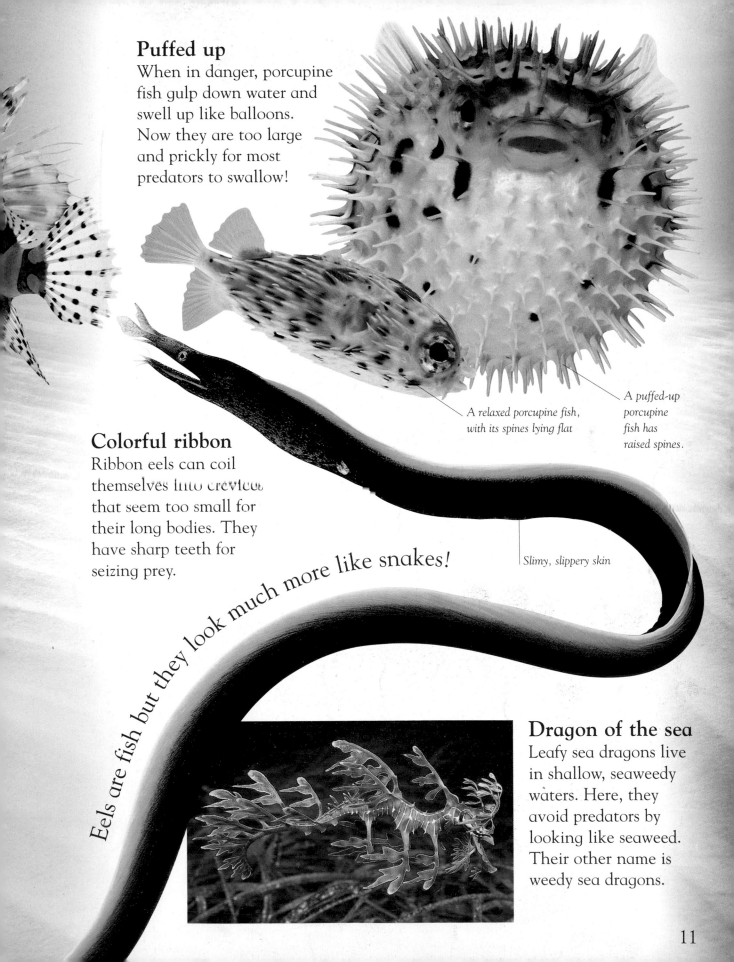

## Puffed up

When in danger, porcupine fish gulp down water and swell up like balloons. Now they are too large and prickly for most predators to swallow!

*A relaxed porcupine fish, with its spines lying flat*

*A puffed-up porcupine fish has raised spines.*

## Colorful ribbon

Ribbon eels can coil themselves into crevices that seem too small for their long bodies. They have sharp teeth for seizing prey.

*Slimy, slippery skin*

*Eels are fish but they look much more like snakes!*

## Dragon of the sea

Leafy sea dragons live in shallow, seaweedy waters. Here, they avoid predators by looking like seaweed. Their other name is weedy sea dragons.

# Jellyfish

Adrift in the oceans since prehistoric times, jellyfish are more than 95 percent water. They have no brains, bones, hearts, or eyes. Their stinging tentacles act like fishing lines to catch prey.

### Dinner is served
Long tentacles trail from the jellyfish's body. When a small animal swims into the tentacles, the jellyfish spears it with poisonous stings.

### OCEAN DRIFTER

In warmer parts of the world, the Portuguese man-of-war drifts on the surface of the waves. It is held up by a balloonlike float. A relative of jellyfish, it is also called blue jellyfish. It catches fish in its long tentacles. These shoot tiny stings into any animal that touches them. People are sometimes stung by Portuguese men-of-war. The stings are not fatal to people, but they are very painful!

### Underwater umbrella
Jellyfish have soft bodies called bells. The bell moves in and out like an umbrella opening and closing. This drives the jellyfish along.

Glowing jellyfish rising to the water's surface on dark nights have been mistaken for ghosts!

*Jellyfish may look like a parachute but they are probably traveling upward!*

## Up, up, and away
Jellyfish are attracted to light even though they have no eyes. They swim toward the water's surface. This keeps them within range of food.

## Fishy words

**Invertebrate** Despite their name, jellyfish are not fish. They are invertebrates. An invertebrate is an animal without a backbone.

**Transparent** A transparent animal or object is one that is see-through.

## Ghostly glow
Many jellyfish are nearly transparent. Some also produce their own light, so that they glow in dark water. They may only do this when disturbed.

# Spectacular sharks

Sharks are survivors! They have lived in the world's oceans since prehistoric times. The largest of all fish, they have muscular bodies, good hearing, and a keen sense of smell for sniffing out food.

## Sleek and streamlined

A strong swimmer, the sandbar shark slices through the ocean at high speed. It swims vast distances, traveling to find food in warmer waters as the seasons change.

## Underwater leopards

Leopard sharks are named for their golden, spotted skin. This is good camouflage on the seabed where they search for their favorite food—clams.

*A hammerhead shark's head is shaped like a hammer.*

## Weird and wonderful

Hammerhead sharks have eyes at each end of their unusual, wide heads. This helps them to see more! Hammerhead sharks like to stick together. There may be as many as 100 of them in a school.

## World's scariest shark
Great whites are the largest carnivorous fish. Seen as ferocious man-eaters, they have been overhunted and are now rare. In fact, great whites do not hunt humans. If they do bite people, they usually spit them out!

*Great whites have more than 100 razor-sharp teeth.*

# Ocean giants

Whales are the largest creatures in the ocean. Like all mammals, they breathe air. Whales take in air through openings called blowholes on their heads. There are two types of whale—baleen whales and toothed whales.

## Splashing around

Humpback whales have longer flippers than other whales. They slap their flippers on the water to make loud splashes. This is called flippering!

## Swimming lesson

A baby whale is called a calf. Humpback calves swim close to their mothers. It takes time for the calf to become a strong swimmer.

## What is a baleen whale?

Humpback whales are baleen whales. Instead of teeth, they have baleen plates. They gulp water and strain it out through the baleen, trapping tiny animals.

## Killer teeth

Killer whales are toothed whales. Small, sharp teeth allow them to grab fish and other prey. Killer whales are also called orcas. They live in social groups called pods.

Leaping out of the water is called breaching.

*Barnacles are small animals with shell-like plates. They often make their homes on whales.*

## The big blue

● The blue whale is not only the largest whale, but also the largest animal of all time.

● The biggest dinosaur was only about a quarter of the weight of a blue whale.

*Blue whale*

*Human*

*Killer whale*

# Playful dolphins

Dolphins are small, toothed whales. Intelligent and curious, they are friendly toward people. They have even rescued shipwreck survivors and helped them back to shore! Speedy swimmers, dolphins race along with long, low leaps. This is called "porpoising."

Dolphins stroke each other with their flippers to make friends.

### Dolphin talk
Using a language of clicks and squeaks, pods of dolphins find their way around the ocean. They organize fish hunts by sending messages to each other. To stun fish, they may make very loud noises!

## Bringing up baby

Dolphins give birth to one calf at a time. The calf drinks its mother's milk and grows quickly. Other dolphins may babysit the calf while its mother hunts for fish.

## Ocean acrobats

Dolphins can leap high out of the water. They may do this to avoid predators or to herd fish by making loud splashes. Males sometimes leap to impress females.

*Curved flippers help dolphins to steer and turn around.*

*The long snout is called a beak.*

*Streamlined body slices through the water.*

### Fishy facts

● Dolphins live in groups called pods. These may join together to form a herd.

● There are dolphins in all the world's oceans, except for icy, polar waters.

● If a dolphin is sick or injured, other dolphins may support it with their bodies so that its blowhole is above the surface.

# Gentle sea cows

In warm, shallow waters, large sea mammals called dugongs and manatees live a peaceful life. They have no natural enemies, eat only plants, and never fight.

Dugongs and manatees lived in the oceans during the age of the dinosaurs.

*Dugongs often dig down into the sand to eat sea grass roots.*

### Funny face
Like manatees, this dugong has no front teeth! Its teeth grow only along the sides of its mouth. Flippers steer and scoop up food.

### Underwater lawnmower
Dugongs and manatees are the only vegetarian sea mammals. They swim slowly, grazing on sea grass.

*Manatees sometimes have algae growing on their backs.*

### Noises in the night
Dugongs relax during the day and spend most of the night eating. Like manatees, they are noisy eaters. There are loud sounds of chomping teeth and flapping lips!

*Sea grass beds are good feeding grounds.*

# Motherly love

Dugongs and manatees give birth to only one calf every three to five years. The newborn calf rises to the surface immediately for its first breath of air. It stays with its mother for up to two years, clinging to her or resting on her back.

*Calf stays close to its mother.*

## Fishy facts

● Dugongs have a tail that is pointed at the ends. Manatees have a paddle-shaped tail.

● On meeting, sea cows grab each other's flippers, then put their mouths together to kiss.

● Manatees and dugongs can live for up to 60 years.

# Soaring seabirds

Some seabirds live along the shore. Others fly far out to sea. All return to the shore to nest. Many nest in groups called colonies. They often choose cliffs, where eggs and chicks are safe from predators.

## In the clouds

A small bird, the Arctic tern flies longer distances than any other bird. It spends most of its life in the air!

*Wing is long and strong.*

## Long-distance flights

Albatrosses fly for weeks at a time. With wings outstretched, they glide through the air. They are carried by the wind and hardly need to bother to flap!

## Sea parrots

Colorful beaks give puffins the nickname "parrots of the sea." Large beaks are useful for grabbing lots of sand eels!

## Birds with big appetites

Pelicans fly or swim in search of a fishy meal. When they spot fish, they dive down after them. They have stretchy beaks for scooping up lots of fish at once.

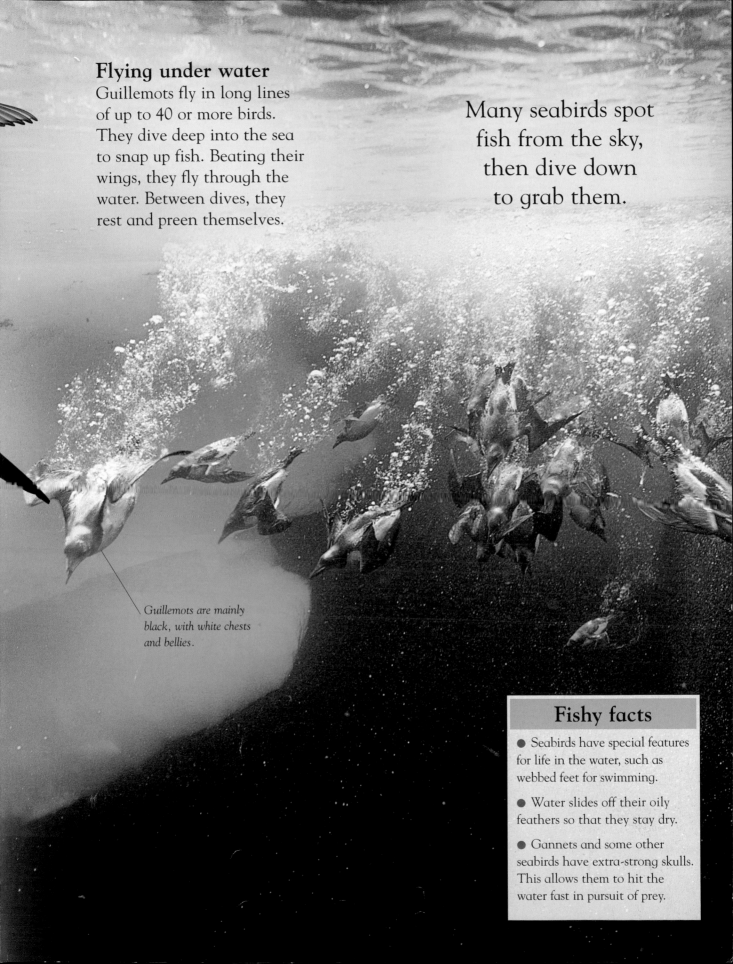

## Flying under water

Guillemots fly in long lines of up to 40 or more birds. They dive deep into the sea to snap up fish. Beating their wings, they fly through the water. Between dives, they rest and preen themselves.

Many seabirds spot fish from the sky, then dive down to grab them.

*Guillemots are mainly black, with white chests and bellies.*

### Fishy facts

● Seabirds have special features for life in the water, such as webbed feet for swimming.

● Water slides off their oily feathers so that they stay dry.

● Gannets and some other seabirds have extra-strong skulls. This allows them to hit the water fast in pursuit of prey.

## Long-distance swimmers

Female green turtles travel to the place where they were born to lay their eggs, then swim back again across the open ocean. With no landmarks to follow, the turtles probably find their way by the positions of the Sun and the Moon.

## Fishy facts

● California gray whales feed in the Arctic Ocean, then travel to warmer waters to breed.

● Arctic terns fly farther than other seabirds, from the North Pole to the South Pole and back.

● Barnacles take long-distance rides on turtles and whales.

# Ocean travelers

Some sea creatures make amazing journeys, crisscrossing the oceans. They travel to find breeding grounds, food, or safety. This is called migration.

*Turtles surface to breathe air through their nostrils.*

## Eels at sea
Eels travel from lakes and rivers to breed at sea. The young eels (elvers) then return to freshwater.

*Broad flippers help turtles to "row" themselves forward.*

## Lobster lineup
To escape storms, spiny lobsters walk along the seabed to calmer waters. They march head to tail. This makes it hard for predators to pick out one.

# Octopuses and squid

Fast hunters, octopuses and squid have long "arms" called tentacles for seizing prey. They swim at high speed by squirting jets of water from their baglike bodies. The force drives them along. This is called jet propulsion.

### Sucker-studded tentacles

Octopuses feel and taste with their eight tentacles. Each tentacle has rows of suckers. The suckers help them to grip prey and fasten themselves to the seabed.

Octopuses are intelligent and have big brains.

## Speedy retreat

When in danger, octopuses jet off.
Their bodies form a torpedolike
shape to slice through water.
Like squid, they can outswim
most predators.

*Tentacles trail out
behind the body as
the octopus takes off.*

## Nighttime prowler

In the daytime, octopuses hide
alone in rocky dens. At night,
they come out to hunt. They
try to keep a tentacle on
the seabed. If threatened,
they can pull themselves
back fast.

## Shimmering squid

Many squid can produce their own light.
They use this light display to signal to each
other or to lure prey. Fire squid can even
flash white, blue, yellow, and red light.

## Ink attack!

To escape predators, octopuses
and squid have a trick up their
sleeves. They squirt out a cloud
of ink. Hidden in murky water,
they make a getaway.

# Living together

Different sea creatures may live together in a variety of fascinating ways. Often the arrangement suits both creatures, but sometimes only one benefits.

*A cleaner wrasse cleans the teeth of a coral trout.*

## Cleaning service

Fish called cleaner wrasse set up cleaning stations in coral reefs. They eat parasites stuck to larger fish. Their customers wait in line. Even natural enemies put aside their differences!

## Perfect partnership

Clown fish escape danger by darting into sea anemones. A coat of slime protects the fish and predators dare not follow.

*Brightly colored clown fish cannot hide easily.*

*Sea anemones have poisonous tentacles.*

*A clown fish's color and pattern warn that the sea anemone is poisonous, so both creatures benefit.*

## Boxing gloves

Boxer crabs carry anemones and wave the stinging tentacles at predators. Anemones eat pieces of food the crabs drop.

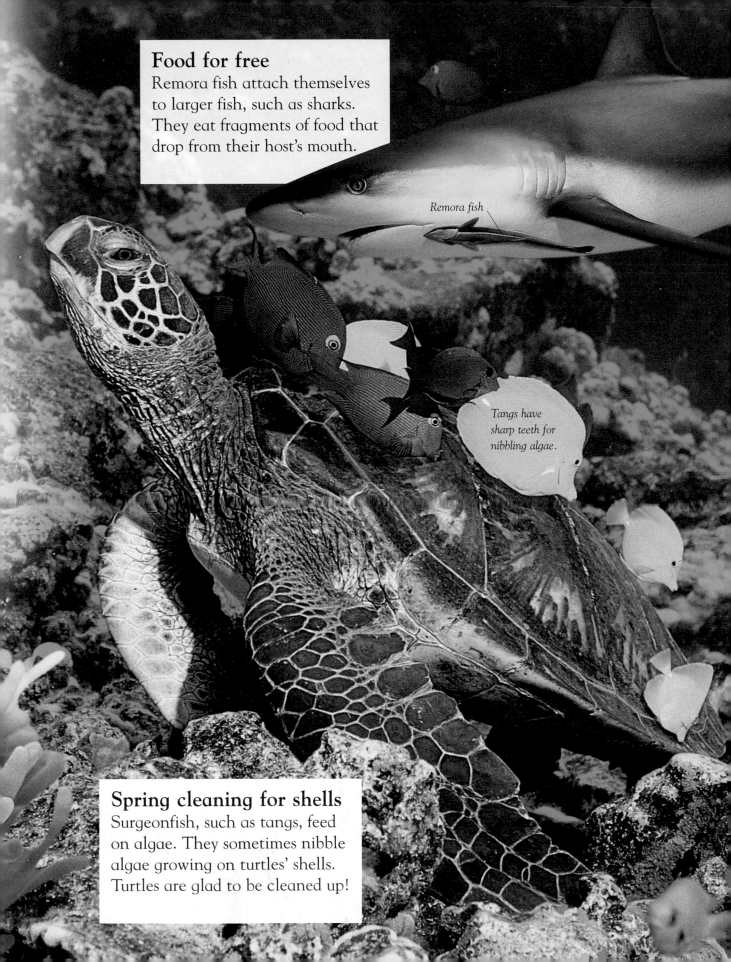

## Food for free
Remora fish attach themselves to larger fish, such as sharks. They eat fragments of food that drop from their host's mouth.

*Remora fish*

*Tangs have sharp teeth for nibbling algae.*

## Spring cleaning for shells
Surgeonfish, such as tangs, feed on algae. They sometimes nibble algae growing on turtles' shells. Turtles are glad to be cleaned up!

# Down in the depths

No light reaches as far down as the ocean's midnight zone. Here, strange creatures live in freezing cold and total darkness. They are small, so they can survive on little food.

*Stretchy stomach expands if the fish lures in a big meal.*

## Angling for fish

Angler fish have a long fishing-rod fin with a light at the end. Small fish think that this is food. Lured toward it, they swim into the angler fish's open jaws.

## Fearsome hunter

The viper fish swims with its jaws open. It catches fish with its extra-long, sharp teeth.

*Mouth has more than 350 lights.*

## Low life

Parts of the ocean floor look like the surface of the Moon. Here, rat-tail fish dart in and out of crevices. It's easy to see how they got their name!

# Ugly ogre

The gruesome looks of the fangtooth explain its other name, "ogre fish." When a fish or shrimp swims past, the fangtooth sucks it into its gigantic mouth.

*Large eye helps the fish to spot prey in the dark.*

*Daggerlike teeth line the fangtooth's huge jaws.*

## Shining like stars

A bladelike, silvery body gives hatchet fish their name. They have light organs along their bellies and tails.

# Life on the seabed

A few seabed animals can survive along the lower seashore. Most live on the deeper seabed, where they are always under water. These creatures often look like plants, but they are really animals.

Sponges can grow so big that a person could have a bath in one!

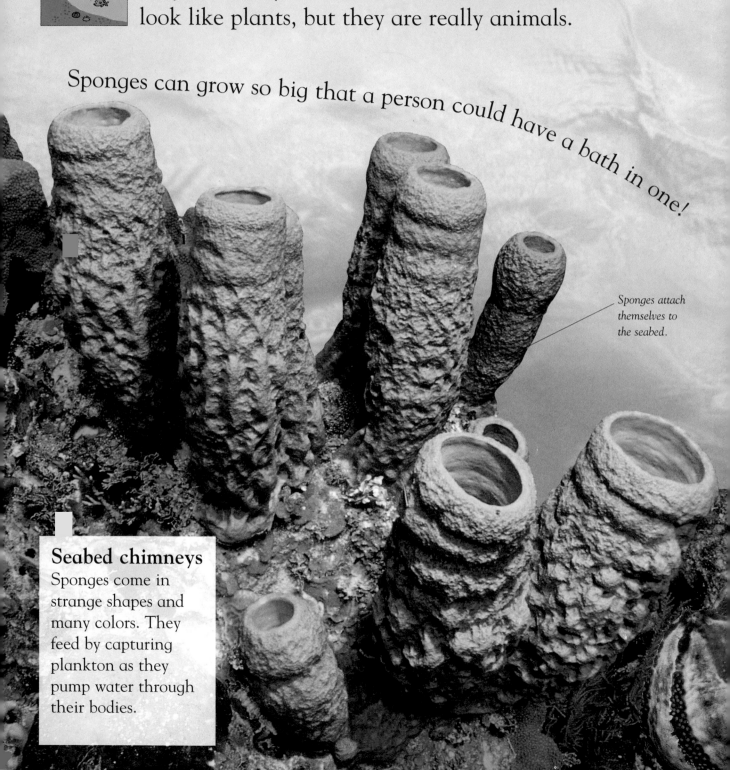

*Sponges attach themselves to the seabed.*

### Seabed chimneys
Sponges come in strange shapes and many colors. They feed by capturing plankton as they pump water through their bodies.

*Spines cover body and arms.*

## Starring role

Brittle stars have brittle, easily broken arms. This does not matter because they can grow new ones! Like starfish, brittle stars do not have brains.

*This common starfish has 12 arms.*

## Hungry starfish

Starfish eat mussels and clams, using the suckers on their feet to pull the shells apart. Then they push their stomachs into the gap and eat up their prey.

*Pair of tentacles helps sea slugs seek out food.*

*Tentacles can be pulled back inside the body.*

*Row of feet*

## In the slow lane

Sea cucumbers crawl along the seabed at a snail's pace. They suck in food that sticks to their slimy tentacles.

## Colorful character

This sea slug is called a "Spanish shawl" because it appears to have an orange fringe. The vivid colors of sea slugs warn predators that they are poisonous and taste awful.

## Fishy facts

● Coral reefs grow in tropical oceans where sea temperature is never below 68°F (20°C).

● Australia's Great Barrier Reef is so large that it can be seen from space.

● New coral reefs will often grow on the seabed wrecks of ships and aircraft.

# Coral reefs

 Coral is built by tiny animals called polyps. Each builds a chalky, cup-shaped shelter to protect its soft body. The reef spreads as young polyps build new shelters on old ones. Different corals form a variety of amazing shapes and colors.

**Organ pipes**
A new layer of coral grows from each tiny pipe of organ-pipe coral.

**Rose coral**
Corals have names that tell you how they look. This coral is like a rose.

*Scallops often make their home in rose coral.*

**Sea fans**
The treelike forms of these corals sometimes join up in the shape of a fan.

**Brain coral**
Brain coral has a grayish color and looks like a human brain!

*Colorful coral reefs look like underwater gardens.*

# Life in a coral reef

Coral reefs teem in the daytime with beautiful and bizarre creatures. At night, many retreat into caves to rest. Now a new party begins! Different fish leave their hideouts to look for food.

**Underwater angels**
With their slim bodies, emperor angelfish can dart in and out of gaps in the coral. Angelfish partners stay together for life.

## SEA SERPENT STORIES

Tales of man-eating sea serpents once made people wary of eels. Today, divers still tell stories of moray eels gripping them in their toothy jaws. Divers mostly have only themselves to blame. Some poke their hands into coral-reef caves. This can give an eel resting at home an unwelcome surprise!

## Lettuce leaf

Like other sea slugs, lettuce slugs are related to garden snails. These frilly slugs may look like salad, but their skin produces a slime that tastes revolting.

Coral reefs offer many hiding places for small fish escaping from larger predators.

## A twist of the tail

To anchor themselves, sea horses twist their tails around corals. If an enemy appears, they change color to match their surroundings.

*Sea horses are among the tiniest fish in a coral reef.*

## Slippery as an eel

Moray eels have slimy, snakelike bodies. They slither into caves and crevices to hide during the day. Their pointed faces peer out from the coral. At night, they hunt for food.

## House-hunting hermits

Hermit crabs often make their homes inside the empty shells of other animals. They may also move into small caves in the coral reef.

# Icy waters

The seas around the North and South poles are partly frozen. Animals that live here have a thick layer of fat, called blubber. This helps to keep them warm.

## Coming up for air
Like all mammals, seals breathe air. They gnaw at sea ice with their sharp teeth to keep air holes open so they can breathe.

*Pups are completely covered in white fur.*

## Snow-white seal pups
Harp seal pups are born with white fur that camouflages them on the ice. This is useful because they often wait alone for their mothers to return from feeding.

Polar bears have black skin under their white fur.

## Noisy walruses
Walruses live in large groups around the North Pole. These noisy animals bark, growl, and whistle to each other. They have two long front teeth called tusks.

*A walrus's tusks can grow up to 3¼ ft (1 m) long.*

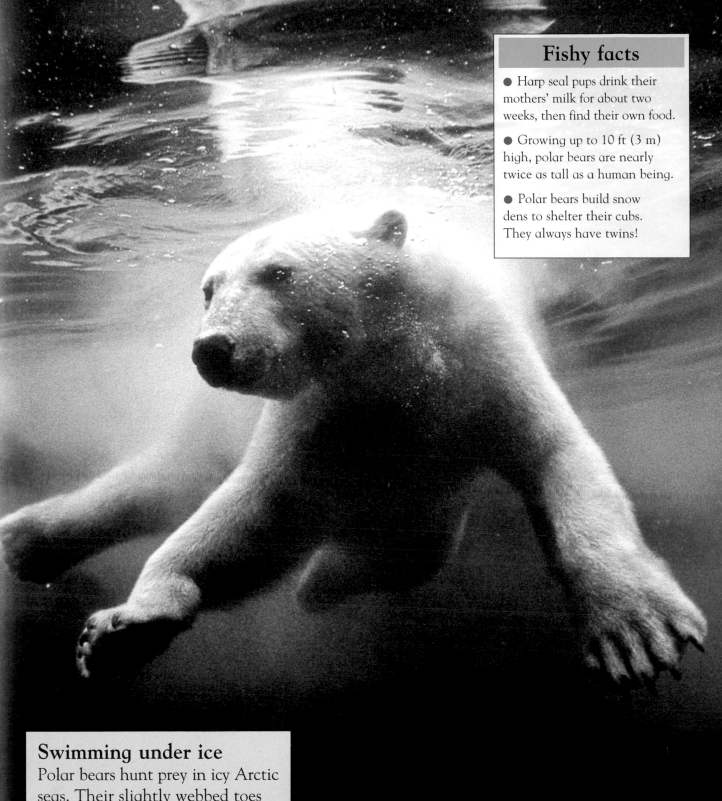

### Swimming under ice

Polar bears hunt prey in icy Arctic seas. Their slightly webbed toes help them to swim. They paddle with their front legs and steer with their hind ones. In the snow, creamy fur is perfect camouflage.

# Penguin party

All penguins live south of the Earth's equator. They have thick fat called blubber to keep them warm in icy waters. Shiny, waterproof feathers prevent their skin from getting wet. They make deep dives to catch fish.

## Daring divers

Adélie penguins are the most common South Pole penguins. They dive into the icy water to hunt for fish and squid. Swimming at high speed, they can launch themselves from the water onto the shore.

*Streamlined shape slices through water.*

*Flipperlike wing rows penguin along under water.*

*Webbed foot has claws.*

### Fishy facts

- Penguins can dive down to about 870 ft (290 m), taking them into the twilight zone.

- The emperor penguin is the largest penguin of all.

- Many penguins live in the coldest, windiest place in the world—the South Pole.

## Making a splash

Penguins are speedy swimmers, but they have no defense against predators. In water, their dark backs and light-colored bellies act as camouflage. This is known as countershading.

Penguins are birds, but they cannot fly. They waddle slowly on land but swim swiftly in the sea.

## Dinnertime

Penguin parents feed their chicks fishy snacks until the chicks can hunt for themselves. Emperor penguin chicks have gray, fluffy feathers. Later, they grow black and white feathers like their parents.

## Perfect parent

After laying eggs, female king penguins return to the sea. Through the icy winter, the males keep the eggs warm on their feet. When the chicks hatch, their mothers reappear to feed them.

## Nursery on the ice

Emperor penguin chicks and adults huddle together in groups of up to 5,000 birds. It is much warmer inside the huddle than outside it. Penguins move around slowly, so that those on the outside have a turn in the middle to warm up!

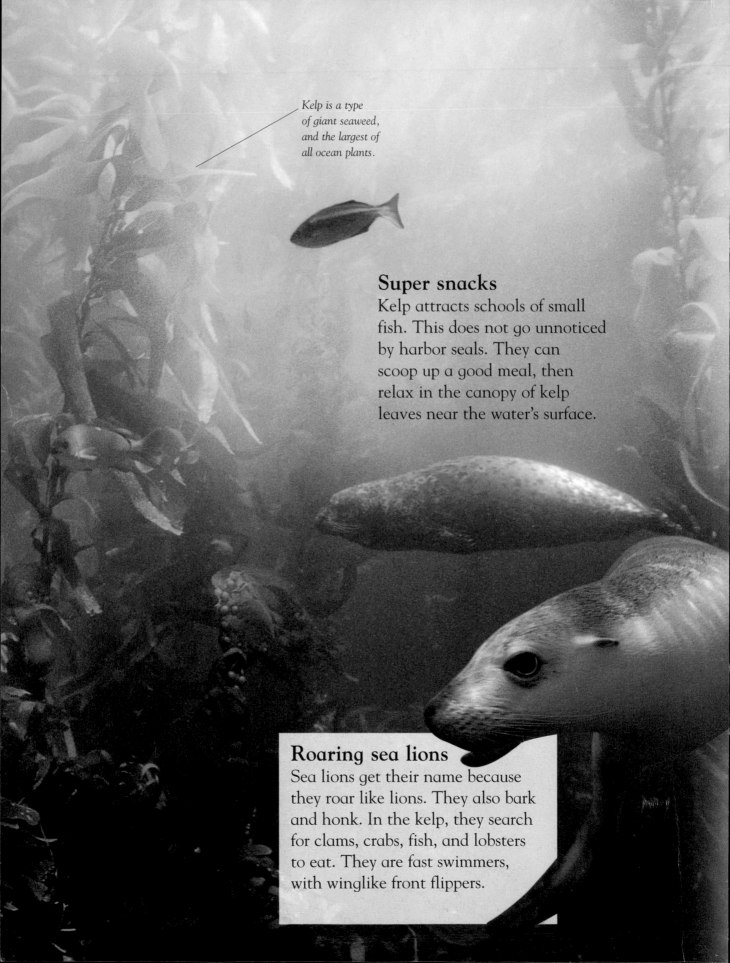

*Kelp is a type
of giant seaweed,
and the largest of
all ocean plants.*

## Super snacks

Kelp attracts schools of small
fish. This does not go unnoticed
by harbor seals. They can
scoop up a good meal, then
relax in the canopy of kelp
leaves near the water's surface.

## Roaring sea lions

Sea lions get their name because
they roar like lions. They also bark
and honk. In the kelp, they search
for clams, crabs, fish, and lobsters
to eat. They are fast swimmers,
with winglike front flippers.

# Kingdom of kelp

Hidden under the waves, kelp forests provide food and shelter for a wealth of creatures. A towering kelp plant is like a high-rise apartment, providing homes for sea creatures at every level.

## Hanging out in hammocks

Sea otters lie in hammocks of kelp. Their waterproof fur is so thick that their skin never gets wet! They use their stomachs as tables for laying out meals.

Some fish graze on the kelp, while others hunt for prey.

## Forest flame

Flame-colored garibaldis have small territories in the kelp. If a neighbor gets too close, the garibaldis confront each other face to face. They wave their tails furiously.

## Shady shark

Horn sharks hunt for sea urchins and shellfish at night. Their eyes are sensitive to light, so they sleep during the day in the shade of large kelp leaves.

*Kelp is attached to the seabed by rootlike anchors called holdfasts.*

# Exploring under water

Oceans have yet to be fully explored. They still have secrets to reveal. To survive under water, divers need special clothing and equipment. Today, they can also travel in underwater machines called submersibles.

## Scuba diving

Scuba (Self-Contained Underwater Breathing Apparatus) allows divers to breathe from tanks of air strapped to their backs.

*Scuba divers study fish and the seabed in shallow waters.*

### BUBBLE TROUBLE

Scuba equipment allows divers to study shallow-water fish in the wild. The problem is that fish, such as hammerhead sharks, are sensitive to the noise made by air bubbles. They may be so scared that they swim away.

## Diving machines

Submersibles are the only way to explore the deep ocean. In them, divers have discovered undersea life never seen before. They are protected from the huge pressure of water that occurs at low levels. The submersible *Nautile* can dive to nearly 20,000 ft (6,000 m).

*Lights for video camera*

*Pilot sits in a metal cabin with a thick, flexible glass window.*

*Submersible is powered to move forward.*

*Diver studying a shipwreck on the seabed*

## Seabed wrecks

Shipwrecks come to rest on the seabed. Scuba divers can explore them in shallow seas. Here, algae and sometimes coral grow on the wrecks as time passes.

## Disaster in the Atlantic

In 1912, the *Titanic* hit an iceberg and sank on its first-ever voyage. The advent of submersibles finally made it possible to explore the wreck. The *Nautile* took nearly two hours to reach it.

# True or false?

Test your knowledge about sea creatures by answering these true or false statements.

**Arctic terns** can only fly short distances.
**See page 22**

All fish have **scales** of the same shape and size.
**See page 9**

**"Scuba"** stands for Self-contained Underwater Breathing Apparatus.
**See page 44**

**Turtles** come to the water's surface to breathe.
**See page 6**

Tangs feed on **algae** growing on sharks.
**See page 29**

Male emperor
penguins keep
**eggs warm**
on their feet.
**See page 40**

**Colorful beaks**
give puffins the
nickname
"peacocks
of the sea."
**See page 22**

Ribbon eels have
**sharp teeth** for
seizing prey.
**See page 11**

Boxer crabs use
**anemones** to
capture prey.
**See page 28**

A **sea horse**
cannot change
its colour.
**See page 37**

The polka-dot grouper
swims **head down** while
searching for food.
**See page 9**

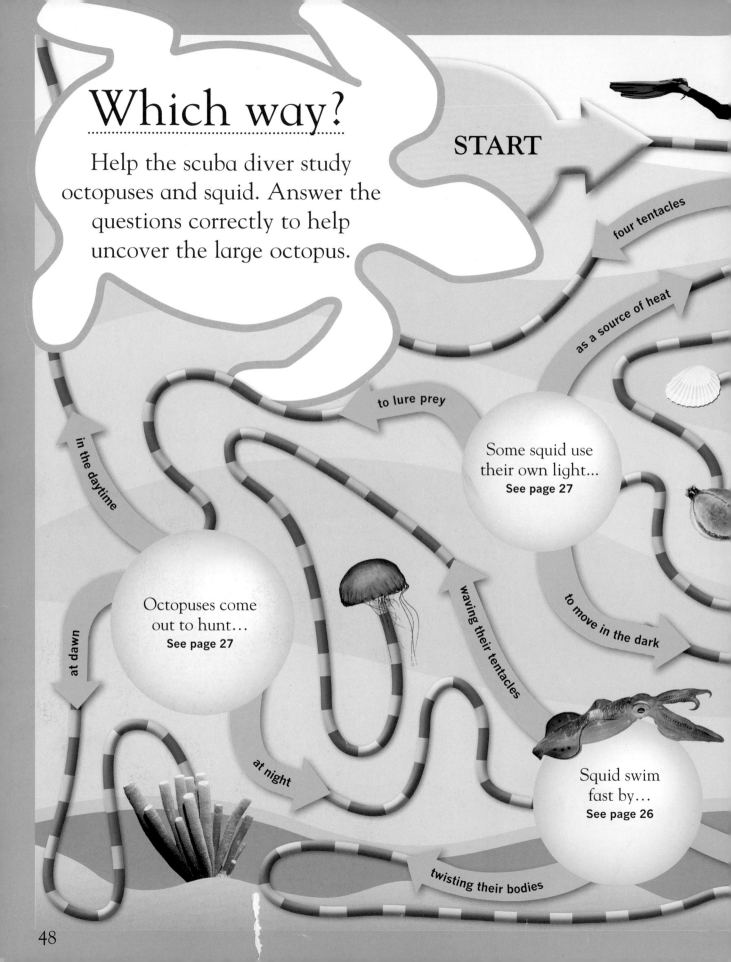

# Which way?

Help the scuba diver study octopuses and squid. Answer the questions correctly to help uncover the large octopus.

START

four tentacles

as a source of heat

to lure prey

in the daytime

Some squid use their own light...
**See page 27**

Octopuses come out to hunt...
**See page 27**

at dawn

waving their tentacles

to move in the dark

at night

Squid swim fast by...
**See page 26**

twisting their bodies

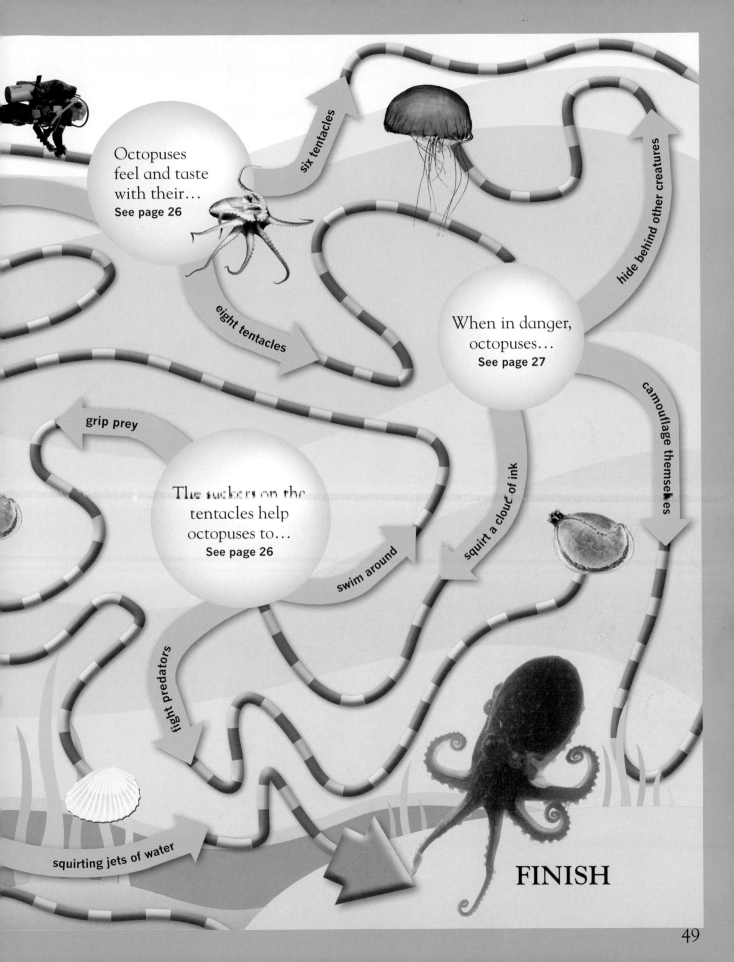

Octopuses feel and taste with their…
**See page 26**

six tentacles

eight tentacles

When in danger, octopuses…
**See page 27**

hide behind other creatures

camouflage themselves

grip prey

The suckers on the tentacles help octopuses to…
**See page 26**

swim around

squirt a cloud of ink

fight predators

squirting jets of water

**FINISH**

# Who am I?

Take a look at these close-ups of animals in the book and see if you can identify them. The clues should help you!

🐟 I have a striped body.

🐟 My poisonous spines will pierce any predator that bites me.

**See page 10**

🐟 I live in a social group called a pod.

🐟 I am a toothed whale.

**See page 17**

🐟 I have spines.

🐟 When threatened, I gulp down water and swell up like a balloon.

**See page 11**

🐟 I change color to look like part of the seabed.

🐟 I have spines on my back for protection.

**See page 10**

🐟 To escape danger, I dart into anemones.

🐟 I am a brightly colored fish.

**See page 28**

🐟 At night, I hunt for sea urchins and shellfish.

🐟 My eyes are sensitive to light.

See page 43

🐟 I am more than 95 percent water.

🐟 I have no brain, bones, heart, or eyes.

See page 12

🐟 I get my name from my bladelike, silvery body.

🐟 I have light organs along my belly and tail.

See page 31

🐟 I have a baglike body.

🐟 I am an intelligent creature with a big brain.

See page 26

🐟 I am related to garden snails.

🐟 My skin produces a slime that tastes revolting.

See page 37

🐟 Tiny animals called polyps build me.

🐟 I look like a human brain.

See page 35

# Facts matchup

Revisit the underwater world. Read the clues below and see if you can find the correct answers among the pictures.

**Leafy sea dragon**

**Kelp**

**Manatee**

**Rose coral**

**Starfish**

**Leopard shark**

**Remora fish**

**Sea otter**

Eyes at each end of my wide head help me to see more. **See page 14**

I crawl along the seabed at a snail's pace. **See page 33**

My wings are long and strong, and I can fly for weeks at a time. **See page 22**

A new layer of coral grows from each of my tiny pipes. **See page 35**

I provide food and shelter for all sorts of sea creatures. **See page 43**

I am a vegetarian mammal. Like the dugong, I have no front teeth. **See page 21**

A coat of slime on my tentacles protects me from predators. See page 28

I get my name from my spotted skin. Clams are my favorite food. See page 14

My waterproof fur is so thick that my skin never gets wet. See page 43

With my slim body, I can dart in and out of gaps in the coral. See page 36

In addition to roaring like a lion, I also bark and honk. See page 42

I live in shallow, seaweedy waters and look like seaweed. See page 11

I pull mussels and clams apart by using the suckers on my feet. See page 33

Dugong

Sea lion

Albatross

Hammerhead shark

Emperor angelfish

Organ-pipe coral

Sea anemone

Sea cucumber

Sponges

We capture plankton and feed on it by pumping water through our bodies. See page 32

I relax during the day and spend most of the night eating. See page 20

Scallops often make their homes in me. See page 35

I attach myself to larger fish, such as sharks. See page 29

# Glossary

**Algae** plants that live in water. They have no roots, stems, or leaves. Seaweed is a sea algae.

**Animal** an animal is any living creature that is not a plant. For example, dolphins, fish, and starfish are animals.

**Antarctic** the cold area around the South Pole that includes the southern parts of the Atlantic, Indian, and Pacific oceans.

**Arctic** the cold area around the North Pole that includes the Arctic Ocean.

**Baleen** baleen is made of the same material as human fingernails. Some whales have baleen plates instead of teeth.

**Blubber** a thick layer of fat that keeps polar animals and whales warm in cold waters.

**Breeding** when animals give birth to young.

**Camouflage** for animals, this is usually skin coloring that makes them look the same as their surroundings. They are then less likely to be attacked.

**Canopy** the topmost layers of leaves in a forest. Kelp forests have a canopy.

**Carnivore** an animal that eats the flesh of another animal.

**Coast** the border of the land where it meets the sea.

**Continental shelf** the shallow part of the seabed around land that ends in a steep slope to the ocean floor.

**Countershading** this is the effect of having a darker back and paler belly. From above, a dark back blends in with the darkness of the deep sea. From below, a pale belly blends in with the light from the sky.

**Crustacean** a type of animal with jointed limbs. Crabs, lobsters, and shrimp are examples of crustaceans.

**Echinoderms** animals with spiny skins and tubed feet. Sea cucumbers, sea urchins, and starfish are echinoderms.

**Equator** an imaginary line around the Earth that is equally distant from the North and the South poles.

**Gills** the part of a fish's body that absorbs oxygen from water so that fish can breathe under water.

**Holdfast** the rootlike anchors attached to kelp.

**Invertebrate** an animal without a backbone.

**Kelp** a type of giant seaweed.

**Luminous** this describes the effect of giving off light. Some fish have light organs that make them luminous.

**Mammal** a warm-blooded animal that breathes oxygen from the air. Female mammals produce milk to feed their young.

**Mollusk** animals that have a soft body and no backbone. Clams, octopuses, sea slugs, and squid are mollusks.

**Oceanography** the study of the oceans is called oceanography.

**Oxygen** a gas that is found in both air and water. All living things need oxygen to breathe.

**Parasite** an animal that lives in, or on, another animal. A parasite benefits at the expense of the other animal.

**Plankton** tiny plants and animals that live in the ocean. They are food for many other, larger sea creatures.

**Polar region** the area near the North Pole or the South Pole.

**Predator** an animal that hunts other animals for food.

**Prey** an animal that is hunted by other animals for food.

**Scale** a small, thin plate. Overlapping scales protect the skin of fish and reptiles.

**Sea** smaller areas of saltwater are called seas. Larger areas of saltwater are called oceans.

**Species** a group of animals or plants made up of related individuals who are able to produce young with one another.

**Seashore** the land along the edge of seas and oceans.

**Streamlined** a smooth shape that allows some sea creatures to travel faster.

**Submersible** a diving machine for exploring the deep ocean.

**Tentacles** long feelers, such as bendable arms, for grasping.

**Territory** an area defended by an animal, or animals, against others of its kind.

# Animal alphabet

Every animal pictured in this book is listed here, along with its page number and the parts of the ocean in which it lives.

# Index

---

# Acknowledgments

**Dorling Kindersley would like to thank:** Hilary Bird for compiling the index, Emily Bolam for original artwork, Penelope York for editorial assistance, and Jon Hughes for additional design work.

# Picture credits

(Key: a = above; b = below; c = center; l = left; r = right; t = top) Dorling Kindersley would like to thank the following for their kind permission to reproduce their photographs/images.

**Alamy Images:** David Cook / blueshiftstudios 46cl; **Bruce Coleman Ltd:** 6c, 11bc; Andrew Purcell 8c, 9r; Charles and Sandra Hood 12r, 43bc; Dr Eckart Pott 41bl; Dr Frieder Sauer 12bl; Fred Bruemmer 38c; Gordon Langsbury 22tr; Hans Reinhard 41br; Jeff Foott 33br, 42c; Joe Mcdonald 6tl; John Cancalosi 22bl; Johnny Johnson 22ac; Mark Carwardine 17tl; Mark Cawardine 7br; Pacific Stock 4c, 14tc, 14br, 14b, 14l, 15c, 16b, 16t, 26c, 27ac, 32t, 33cr, 42br, 44c, 54c; Steven C Kaufman 38br. **Dorling Kindersley:** Frank Greenaway 14cl; The Natural History Museum, London 52c, 53cl, The Weymouth Sea Life Centre 50crb; Jerry Young 56tr. **Dreamstime.com:** Adeliepenguin 47tl,

Cruskoko 52cl, Cynoclub 52tr, Inga Ivanova 48crb, Dirk-jan Mattaar 48bl, Rick Sargeant 48cb, 49tc, Teguh Tirtaputra 47clb, Kim Worrell 52crb; **Fotolia:** Chrispo 46tc, Nataly-Nete 46bl, Stefan Zeitz / Lux 47tr; **Robert Harding Picture Library:** John Warden 39c. **N.H.P.A.:** 13cl; Bill Wood 28tl; Norbert Wu 29tl; Robert Wu 30tl. **Oxford Scientific Films:** David B. Fleetham 13tr, 20cl; Doug Allan 23c; Herb Segars 12tl; Howard Hall 12br, 13t, 18c, 25br; Konrad Wothe 19tr; Laurence Gould 45c; Paul Kay 32b; Peter Parks 30clb; Tamy Peluso 27br; Tobias Bernhard 20cr. **Photoshot:** Image Quest 3-D / NHPA 51tc, 51br; **Pictor International:** 4l. **Planet Earth Pictures:** 34c, 35bc, 35r, 36c, 37r; A. Kerstitch 33tl; Ashley J. Boyd 37b; David Seiferi 18bl; Doug Perrine 29c; Gary Bell 2l, 3r, 28bl; Mark Conlin 20b; Norbert Wu 31bc, 43ac; Pieter Folkens 38tr; Tom Walker 17tr. **Science Photo Library:** Art Wolfe 40c, 41tr; Douglas Faulkner 21c; F.S. Westmorland 1c. **Southampton Oceanography Centre:** 30b. **gettyone stone:** George Lepp 22br. **Telegraph Colour Library:** 10c.

All other images © Dorling Kindersley
For further information see: www.dkimages.com

**Useful website addresses:**
EnchantedLearning.com/subjects/ocean; www.aqua.org;
www.underwater.com.au; www.ocean.udel.edu/deepsea/